LET'S CELEBRATE

SUMMER

WORLD FESTIVALS

Rhoda Nottridge

Wayland

Other titles in this series include:

Let's Celebrate Spring
Let's Celebrate Autumn
Let's Celebrate Winter

Editor: Deb Elliott
Designer: Helen White

Cover: (top left) A statue of an Inca sun god, used in festivals in Colombia, South America. (top right) All dressed up for a summer carnival. (bottom left) A young girl in make-up and costume for the Notting Hill Carnival in London, England. (bottom right) A firework display in Sydney celebrating Australia Day.

Text is based on *Summer Festivals* in the *Seasonal Festivals* series published in 1990.

First published in 1994 by
Wayland (Publishers) Limited
61 Western Road, Hove
East Sussex, BN3 1JD, England

British Library Cataloguing in Publication Data
Nottridge, Rhoda
Summer. - (Let's Celebrate Series)
I. Title II. Series
394.2

ISBN 0 7502 1178 4

Typeset by White Design
Printed and bound by Casterman S.A. in Belgium

CONTENTS

4 SUMMERTIME

6 SUMMER STARTS

8 MAY DANCES

10 MAY HOLIDAY

12 DRAGON BOAT FESTIVAL

14 SUN FESTIVALS

16 O-BON FESTIVAL

18 FESTIVAL OF HUNGRY GHOSTS

20 BASTILLE DAY

22 INDEPENDENCE DAY

24 FREEDOM AND FESTIVALS

26 WELSH EISTEDDFODS

28 CARNIVALS

30 GLOSSARY

31 BOOKS TO READ

32 INDEX

SUMMERTIME

In the summer the sun shines and the weather is warm. The sun rises early in the morning and sets late in the evening. Most people enjoy the summertime. It is warm and they can spend more time outdoors. They might have picnics or play outdoor sports or visit the countryside. Some people go on holiday.

BELOW *In the summer sunflowers grow so quickly that they can become taller than people.*

LEFT When the weather feels hot and sticky in the summer there are sometimes storms with thunder and lightning.

BELOW The summer sun has ripened the grapes. They are being picked ready for us to eat.

Lots of fruit and vegetables and other crops ripen in the sunshine.

People celebrate the power of the sun with wonderful outdoor festivals. There are also many special events that have happened during summers in the past. People like to celebrate those events.

SUMMER STARTS

Many years ago in Europe people divided the year into two seasons, instead of four. The two seasons were summer and winter. Summer started on 1 May each year. Everyone celebrated with big bonfires and a festival.

BELOW In an Austrian village all the men help to put up the maypole.

ABOVE Children hold the coloured ribbons and dance around the maypole to celebrate summer.

People still celebrate the beginning of summer on 1 May. They continue old traditions. In some countries in Europe people dance round a maypole. A maypole is the trunk of a tree. It is decorated and put in the centre of the village.

MAY DANCES

ABOVE Morris dancing is very popular on May Day.

May Day dances used to be performed mainly by women. Now children often do the dances. Men perform Morris dances. These are supposed to frighten away the evil ghosts of winter and bring a good summer.

Morris dancers wear special hats and clothes decorated with bells and leaves. When they dance they bang sticks together and clap their hands and stamp their feet. One man dresses up in a special animal costume. He is called the hobby-horse.

BELOW *The hobby-horse man takes part in a May Day parade in Britain.*

MAY HOLIDAY

Many years ago there were a lot of changes in the way people lived in Europe. Factories were opened to build new machines. People moved from the countryside to work in the factories. The towns were filled with smoke and dust. People had to work long hours without proper holidays.

BELOW The May Day holiday gave people who worked in factories a day away from the smoke and dirt.

ABOVE May Day celebrations in China include fireworks.

Nearly 100 years ago, a large group of workers decided that everyone should have a holiday on 1 May. Nowadays 1 May is a special day for workers in many countries. People have special parades and remember how important it is to look after workers properly and give them holidays.

DRAGON BOAT FESTIVAL

ABOVE Boats are decorated to look like dragons for the Chinese dragon boat festival.

Many thousands of years ago there was a poet called Chu Yuan who lived in China. He gave the Chinese rulers wise advice but they did not listen to him. He threw himself into a river as a protest.

The local people raced to try and save him. All the dragons and wicked ghosts that lived in the lake wanted to eat Chu Yuan's body. The people could not save Chu Yuan but they threw rice dumplings into the water to keep the greedy dragons away from the body.

All the people were sad when they heard about Chu Yuan's death. Now each year there is a dragon boat festival. Boat races are held to remember the race to save Chu Yuan.

BELOW *The dragon boat races are very popular.*

SUN FESTIVALS

RIGHT This special gold mask of a sun god is very old. It was made by the Inca people who used to live in South America.

BELOW In South America, the Incas and Aztec people worshipped the sun. They believed that it protected them from evil. The people had dances and prayers and gave offerings to the sun god.

ABOVE In Britain the Druids celebrated midsummer at a special festival at Stonehenge.

In Europe people also celebrated the power of the sun at midsummer. This is the longest day of the year, when it stays light for a long time. In Britain the people who celebrated the sun were called Druids.

O-BON FESTIVAL

ABOVE During O-bon food is put aside at each meal for the ghosts to enjoy.

For Japanese Buddhists O-bon is an important summer festival. It is a time when everyone remembers the dead. O-bon lasts for three days.

RIGHT On the second day of O-bon special dances are performed.

On the first day of the festival the family tidies the dead peoples' graves. Then the family goes home and puts fresh herbs and flowers in the house to welcome the ghosts.

The second day of the festival begins with everyone thinking about the ghosts. Later in the day there is a big meal which is often shared with other families. On the last day of the festival, fires are lit. These are to guide the ghosts home again.

FESTIVAL OF HUNGRY GHOSTS

This Chinese summer festival also remembers the dead. It is called the festival of hungry ghosts because it remembers all the unhappy ghosts who may not have families to remember them or they may have died and not had proper funerals.

If nobody is kind to the ghosts then they cause trouble for the living. So they are offered gifts such as pretend paper money and food. The paper presents are burned and the flames carry them to the ghosts. Some Buddhists build paper boats which are burned. They believe the boats help ghosts cross a sea of pain to find a peaceful place to rest.

Boats are also used in a Japanese festival called Miyazu Toro Naghi. People float lanterns in the shape of boats on the sea. The evening tide carries them out to sea. The story goes that the lanterns help the ghosts of drowned sailors to find their way home.

RIGHT *Paper offerings are burned at a grave in Malaysia to keep the hungry ghosts happy.*

BASTILLE DAY

ABOVE *This drawing shows French people attacking the hated Bastille prison over 200 years ago.*

In some countries people celebrate their independence in the summer. Many wars have been fought in the past by people who wanted to be free of bad rulers.

In France around 200 years ago, many people were very unhappy. They did not have enough to eat and yet the king and queen were very rich.

If anyone complained they were sent to the Bastille prison. The people became very angry. On 14 July they attacked the Bastille and set free all the prisoners.

This was the beginning of a struggle by the French people to get rid of the king and queen and choose their own rulers. The people won their fight and to this day everyone remembers Bastille Day. They celebrate their independence with a day's holiday.

BELOW *French people still celebrate the fall of the Bastille on the 14 July.*

INDEPENDENCE DAY

LEFT *These men signed a paper which said that the USA was free from British rule.*

Many wars to get independence are fights against foreign rulers. Over 200 years ago, people living in the USA were ruled by the British. The Americans wanted to rule themselves. On 4 July, 1776 the American people told the British that they could no longer rule them.

RIGHT *Every year on 4 July there are fireworks in the USA to celebrate Independence Day.*

There was a war but the Americans won and set up their own government. Now every year 4 July is a holiday. There are big parades and lots of parties. It is called Independence Day.

In Canada people celebrate independence from British rule on the first Monday of July. They also have parades and parties.

LEFT The Statue of Liberty in New York was given to the USA by the French people. For Americans it is a sign of their freedom.

FREEDOM AND FESTIVALS

Many countries celebrate gaining independence from foreign rulers.

In Australia, the 26 January is called Australia Day. Some Australians celebrate the arrival of the British people who ruled Australia. Although this festival is in January it is summertime in Australia.

BELOW This Australia Day event remembers the arrival of the first Europeans in Australia.

ABOVE Maoris in New Zealand continue to keep their traditions alive with festivals.

In New Zealand there is a celebration of the end of the war between the Maori people and the Europeans who had decided to live there.

Some of these celebrations make people think about their rulers today. For Australian Aborigines Australia Day is celebrating a time when Europeans stole Aboriginal land. Independence days can make people think about whether their rulers are fair to all people.

WELSH EISTEDDFODS

ABOVE *At an eisteddfod people wear their national costumes and do traditional dances.*

An eisteddfod is a Welsh festival of music, dance and poetry. A similar kind of festival is held in Ireland. It is called a feis. These festivals were started many hundreds of years ago by the Celtic people.

At an eisteddfod there are lots of competitions to find the best writers and performers. People speak the Welsh language and wear costumes and continue old traditions. There are lots of eisteddfods in the summer and at one of them people come from around the world to compete in dance and music competitions.

BELOW *There is a special eisteddfod held just for young people.*

CARNIVALS

Carnivals are special parades. They are held in January or February in places like Brazil and the Caribbean.

When people came to live in Britain from the Caribbean they found that their festival was in the middle of winter. It was too cold to have a parade.

BELOW *Carnivals include a parade with everyone dressed up.*

LEFT People spend weeks making beautiful costumes for the carnival.

Some people from the Caribbean who lived in London in the 1960s decided to change their old carnival date and have it in August instead. Then it would be nice and warm. Now it is held in London every year in a place called Notting Hill. There is a big parade and there are wonderful floats. There are parties in the street and the Caribbean traditions are continued.

GLOSSARY

Aborigines The original people living in Australia.
advice Ways of trying to help people with ideas.
crops The food we grow.
dumplings Small balls or parcels of rice or flour with fillings.
events Special times or occasions which are different to usual times.
funeral A ceremony or event for a dead person.
government The people who are chosen to rule a country.
Maoris The original people living in New Zealand.
offerings Special presents given to people or gods.
parades Special marches or processions.
performed An event or show which is staged in front of people.
protest A way of showing that you disagree with something.
ripened When fruit or vegetables are ready to be eaten.
traditions Special customs or ceremonies that people have done for many years.
trunk The main, central part of a tree.

BOOKS TO READ

Get Set Go! In Summer by Ruth Thomson (Franklin Watts,1993)

People and Customs in the *Look It Up* series (Heinemann, 1992)

Poems for Summer selected by Robert Hull (Wayland, 1990)

Summer edited by Daphne Butler (Simon & Schuster, 1992)

The Weather in Summer by Miriam Moss (Wayland, 1994)

Picture acknowledgements
Celtic Picture Agency 26, 27; Eye Ubiquitous 8, 9, 19; Mary Evans Picture Library 15, 20; Sally & Richard Greenhill 13; Hutchison Library 14 (left); Life File cover (bottom right and left); The Mansell Collection 10; Tony Morrison cover (top), 14 (right); Christine Osborne/Middle East Pictures 4, 28; Photri 6, 16, 22 (both), 23, 25; Spectrum Colour Library 24; Topham Picture Library 5 (right), 11, 21; Tim Woodcock 7; Zefa cover (top right), 12, 29.

INDEX

Australia Day 24

Bastille Day (in France) 20-21

carnivals
- in Brazil 28
- in the Caribbean 28
- Notting Hill 29

Chinese celebrations
- dragon boat festival 12-13
- festival of hungry ghosts 18

countryside 4, 10

druids 15

freedom festivals
- in Africa 24
- in Australia 24
- in India 24
- in New Zealand 25

independence celebrations
- in Canada 23
- in France 20-21
- in the USA 22-3

Japanese celebrations
- Miyazu Toro Naghi 18
- O-bon 16-17

Malaysia 19

May Day celebrations
- in Austria 6
- in Britain 9
- in China 11

morris dancing 8

sun festivals
- in Britain 15
- in northern Europe 15
- in South America 14

weather in summer 4